# In the Stillness

## 40 DAYS OF POEMS FOR THE ONE LEARNING TO ABIDE

STACY BRANTNER

In the Stillness.

Print ISBN: 978-1-968889-05-0
Digital ISBN: 978-1-968889-06-7
LCCN: 9781968889050

Cover and Interior Design by Nelly Murariu at PixBeeDesign.com
Manuscript Edits by Market Refined Media & Publishing

Printed in the United States of America
First Edition: September 2025

# Dedication

To all at The Summit of Fort Payne—
where I found the hope of Jesus Christ
that healed my broken heart.

*"To grant to those who mourn in Zion—
to give them a beautiful headdress instead
of ashes, the oil of gladness instead of
mourning, the garment of praise instead
of a faint spirit; that they may be called
oaks of righteousness, the planting of
the LORD, that He may be glorified."*

Isaiah 61:3

# His Sanctuary

The Summit is a special place
set apart as holy ground.
It's where souls are saved and lives are changed,
it's where peace and hope are found.
The ladies who have entered here
were living life deluded;
each one broken in her own way
but all wanting to feel included.
And God, who is our refuge,
brought us to His sanctuary,
taking us from the enemy,
the evil adversary.
Our ashes are turned to beauty,
our morning is turned to joy.
Now we are called trees of righteousness
that can never be destroyed.
Jesus Christ has set us free
from the life we lived in sin.
The Summit in Fort Payne
is where healing in Christ begins.
Jesus is our Savior.
He is truly our only need
and those who are set free by the Lord
are truly free indeed.

# Table of Contents

# Note from the Author

These poems are all based off the hope I found in God's Word. In every trial that I've faced, I found all that I needed through Scripture. These poems are a reflection of those trials.

---

# DAY 1

---

## *Today's Verse*

"Be still and know that I am God." Psalm 46:10

## *Pause and Pray*

There is so much to be learned just by being still. Help us to see You in the stillness.

# In the Stillness

In the stillness
from above
is my God's
unfailing love.
When I seek Him,
I always find
that love is patient
and love is kind.
Now when I'm tossed
about to sea,
I feel His hand
calm the storm in me.
There is a purpose
for my pain;
once I thought I'd lost
but I have really gained.
He's taught me how
to stand on faith.
He gives me mercy,
He gives me grace.
My struggle is never
left unheard.
I find all my answers
in His Word.

# DAY 2

## *Today's Verse*

"Therefore, my beloved, as you have always obeyed, so now, not only as in my presence but much more in my absence, work out your own salvation with fear and trembling." Philippians 2:12

## *Pause and Pray*

You, Lord, are our salvation. May we honor You in all things, because all things are from You.

# Until My Troubles Fade Away

I looked up at the sky today—
such a beautiful shade of blue—
and as I stood there, I began to weep
because I was waiting for You.
I wondered what it will be like,
the day You will appear.
Will I stand in speechless awe,
or will I shout and cheer?
For on that day my troubles will fade
and they will be no more,
for You are the conqueror of this world
and You are coming with a mighty sword.
But before that day comes to pass,
I will stand right here,
working out my salvation
with trembling and fear.

# DAY 3

## *Today's Verse*

"Do not hide your face from me in the day of my distress! Incline your ear to me; answer me speedily in the day when I call!" Psalm 102:2

## *Pause and Pray*

Help us to stay focused even in the silence, searching our hearts completely for why this might be so.

# No Answers

What does it mean when I wake each morning
and Your face I cannot see?
What does it mean when I have no answers?
Why have You hidden Your face from me?
I keep pushing through each day,
and I keep calling on Your name.
For I know Your love is with me
each and every day the same.
So, God, I thank you for this trial,
whether it's a long or little while.
Keep me in Your perfect peace.
Please hold me close; do not release.
Always pull me deeper still,
keeping me always inside Your will.

# DAY 4

*Today's Verse*

"The LORD will fight for you, and you have only to be silent." Exodus 14:14

*Pause and Pray*

In our times of trouble, we need not say a word. The Lord is already there to help us in our time of trouble. May we leave all things in His hands.

# Fighting Silently

He sees the tears
running down your face,
and He puts each one
in a special place.
I know it's hard
when you don't want to try.
But He's looking down,
so look up to the sky.
No trouble is too big.
No worry is too small.
For He is a mighty God.
He can handle them all.
Never give up,
no matter what you do.
It's when you're silent
that He's fighting for you.

---

# DAY 5

---

## *Today's Verse*

"My grace is sufficient for you, for my power is made perfect in weakness." 2 Corinthians 12:9

## *Pause and Pray*

Give us grace to draw from Your strength when we are weak.

# The Perfect Power

What is on your mind?
What has you feeling weak?
In these times of trouble,
whose face do you seek?
His grace is more than sufficient,
and He gives it all to you.
His mercies are unending.
We both know this much is true.
So when you're at your weakest
and you feel you can't go on,
sit at the feet of Jesus,
for it's He who makes you strong.
He is mightier than mighty
and He will always call you friend.
His power is made perfect
when you feel you've reached the end.

---
# DAY 6
---

## *Today's Verse*

"Under the whole heaven he lets it go, and his lightning to the corners of the earth. After it his voice roars; he thunders with his majestic voice, and he does not restrain the lightnings when his voice is heard. God thunders wondrously with his voice; he does great things that we cannot comprehend." Job 37:3-5

## *Pause and Pray*

From the moment we wake and throughout the rest of our day, may we see You and Your glory in everything we do.

# Notice Me

I woke you gently this morning,
I kissed your face with sun.
The grass had been kissed by dew,
your day had just begun,
but you did not notice Me.
I sent a breeze to cool you
as the day went by.
I even put My promise
of the rainbow in the sky.
But you did not notice Me.
I darkened the sky above you
and called with a thunderous roar.
The rain fell on your face
and it cooled you to the core,
but you did not notice Me.
I sent My Son to die
on the cross at Calvary.
What more will it take
for you to notice Me?

# DAY 7

## *Today's Verse*

"Behold, I stand at the door and knock. If anyone hears my voice and opens the door, I will come in to him and eat with him, and he with me." Revelation 3:20

## *Pause and Pray*

Thank You, Lord, for being a long-suffering gentleman who waited so patiently for me.

# Waiting for Me

I search my whole life through
not knowing what more I could do.
I searched in places,
I searched in faces,
and I couldn't see
You were waiting for me.
What kind of love that must be!
You were waiting for me.
I was in such despair,
drowning out every single care.
I was broken and hurting
and my heart was yearning
for someone to see
and You were still waiting for me.
What kind of love that must be!
You are waiting for me.
But when I hit my lowest place
with the enemy in my face,
when nothing else mattered
and my world was shattered
and I couldn't breathe,
*"Behold, I stand at the door and knock,*
    *if anyone hears My voice and opens the door,*
*I will come into him and eat with him,*
    *and he with Me."*
You had been waiting for me.
I was blind but now I can see
You were waiting for me.

What kind of love that must be!
Jesus waited for me
and now I can't wait
for that glorious day
when all is made new.
I am now here
with nothing to fear
and I am waiting for You.

*"Fill me with Your Spirit,
encourage me with Your
love, restore me back to joy
that only comes from above."*

- I Want to Look Like You

# DAY 8

## *Today's Verse*

"Be strong and courageous. Do not be frightened, and do not be dismayed, for the LORD your God is with you wherever you go." Joshua 1:9

## *Pause and Pray*

When our trials make us weary, may we walk victoriously and fearlessly, drawing on Your strength, knowing you walk right beside us every step of the way.

# Limitless

We face so many trials
all along the way
and distractions from the enemy
who tries to steal each day.
And if we are not careful
to lean on the promises of God,
we will all grow weary
while walking on this sod.
So when we feel our walls
crushing from every side,
we must draw near to Him
because He has never lied.
We never walk alone.
Our Lord is always there,
molding us and making us
with tender compassionate care.
So when it feels too hard,
hold your head up high,
knowing that in the hard times,
God still reins on high.
He's looking down from heaven,
He sees all we're going through.
But even in the hard times
there's nothing He can't do.

---

# DAY 9

---

## Today's Verse

"No longer do I call you servants, for the servant does not know what his master is doing; but I have called you friends, for all that I have heard from my Father I have made known to you." John 15:15

## Pause and Pray

We live in a fallen world; therefore, friends will always let us down. Jesus never will. He calls us His friends, making Him the best friend we can have.

# My Best Friend

There have been many friends
I've had throughout my life.
With some, I could share every happiness.
With some, every single strife.
All have come and gone,
leaving a hole inside my heart.
I always dread a new beginning
because I never know just where to start.
But then I met my best friend
who died to set me free,
mending every single hole,
proving His love for me.
I share with Him my joy
and I tell Him all my sorrows.
I talk to Him about today
and I talk to Him about tomorrow.
He knows my every weakness
that brings me to my knees,
and when I'm flying high
He celebrates my victories.
He walks right by my side,
He wipes away all my tears.
He loves me unconditionally,
taking away all my fears.
It is because of my best friend
that I never walk alone.
He is more than special—
He sits on heaven's throne!

I will always love Him
He's given me a new heart.
From my very best friend
I will never have to part.
When you read His story,
know that every word is true.
The best part is my best friend
longs to be your best friend too.

*"God, I pray for Your protection to guard me through all my days. I pray for You to light my path and keep me on the narrow way."*

- Everywhere I Go

---
# DAY 10
---

## Today's Verse

"Do not be anxious about anything, but in everything by prayer and supplication with thanksgiving let your requests be made known to God. And the peace of God, which surpasses all understanding, will guard your hearts and your minds in Christ Jesus."

Philippians 4:6-7

## Pause and Pray

When worry comes—as it is sure to do—may we rest each night with thankful hearts, leaving every care with You and trusting that You already have everything worked out for us.

# As I Sleep

Sometimes I feel so weak
and I'm not sure what to do.
But in Your Word, I'm told
to cast my cares on You.
I wish that I could say
that I trust You with all my heart.
But to tell the truth, dear Lord,
inside I'm falling apart.
Please always hold me close
and always draw me near.
Please grant the peace I read about
and take away my fear.
Watch over me as I sleep tonight.
Guard each and every dream.
Lord, please, bind the hands of Satan
and all his evil schemes.
So now You know my heart—
You know all my anxieties too.
Please make tomorrow easier,
I'm choosing to lean on You.

# DAY 11

## *Today's Verse*

"Likewise the Spirit helps us in our weakness.
For we do not know what to pray for as we ought,
but the Spirit himself intercedes for us with
groanings too deep for words." Romans 8:26

## *Pause and Pray*

Thank You for Your Spirit, Lord, who brings
everything we pray to You the way You need to
hear it when we don't have the words.

# Send Your Spirit

I come to You again tonight,
still struggling with this same old fight.
I'm calling on Your name again
because You said You are my friend.
You told me I don't need to worry
for You have written my entire story.
But God you know the devil is so bold,
sometimes his antics are hard to hold.
On this night I choose to release,
I'm begging You to restore my peace.
Please forgive me of my unbelief.
Only You can stop this kind of grief.
So, on this night when I cannot speak
I need your Spirit, for I am weak.

# DAY 12

### Today's Verse

"We are afflicted in every way, but not crushed;
perplexed, but not driven to despair; persecuted,
but not forsaken; struck down, but not destroyed;
always carrying in the body the death of Jesus,
so that the life of Jesus may also be manifested in
our bodies." 2 Corinthians 4:8-10

### Pause and Pray

When life seems to spin out of control and the pain is
more than we think we can bare, may we put our trust
in You, knowing that you share in everything we are
going through.

# Choose To Trust the Lord

At the Feet of Jesus
there is so much I can see.
He bore all my sins
but there's so much more He did for me.
He took on all my sorrow.
In my grief He surely shares,
and in my weakest moments
He's shown me how much He cares.
When I am perplexed
and not sure how to cope,
He's praying to the Father
that I will not lose hope.
I reached out for His garment
when I was on my knees,
and as I worshipped Him
my pain began to ease.
Things are not completely better
and I'm not sure what this was for,
but in my weakest moments
I choose to trust the Lord.

---
# DAY 13
---

*Today's Verse*

> "But Jesus looked at them and said, 'With man this is impossible, but with God all things are possible.'"
>
> Matthew 19:26

*Pause and Pray*

When things look impossible, may we always look to the One who can make all things possible.

# Look Up

Dangling from a cliff,
suspended in thin air,
we see the rocks below—
we think that no one cares.
There's nothing but despair
at this moment in time.
If the rope should break
we'd be dead on a dime.
The fall is far too long,
the rocks are far too fatal,
but with one turn of our head
we can see the One who's able
to take our situation
and turn it completely around,
doing the impossible,
getting us safely back to ground.
We must always have faith
in the One we are tethered to.
We are all in Christ.
We must trust what He can do.
He takes us through every trial
He always sees us through
Let's always look to Christ.
There's nothing He can't do.

---
# DAY 14
---

## *Today's Verse*

"In the same way, let your light shine before others,
so that they may see your good works and give glory
to your Father who is in heaven." Matthew 5:16

## *Pause and Pray*

When we want insanity to stop, help us to stop
the insanity.

# Changing Me

In a world that is spinning
completely out of control,
the Holy Spirit groans
within our very soul.
There's so much evil in the world
leading to despair.
It's hard not to wonder,
Does anybody care?
But what if we would stop
several times a day
and offer just a smile
to someone along the way?
Or how about showing kindness—
that's what we're called to do.
If we want to change the world
we must start with me and you.
Simple acts of kindness
are so contagious, you see!
I want to change the world,
so I will start with changing me.

# DAY 15

## *Today's Verse*

"Come to me, all who labor and are heavy laden, and I will give you rest." Matthew 11:28

## *Pause and Pray*

Thank you, Lord, for Your promise to take our load when it is more than we can bear and give us rest when we are weary.

# Come to Me

When I'm weary
with no sign of hope,
when my burdens are heavy
and I cannot cope,
I hear a voice whisper:
"You can Come to Me.
Let Me help you.
Your pain will ease.
I'll comfort you
and take your pain,
restore your hope,
make you whole again.
I know it's hard.
There are lots of tests,
so come to Me.
You'll find your rest.
In every struggle,
in every trial,
I will be with you
to walk each mile.
I will not leave you.
You're not alone,
just rest in Me.
No need to roam.
I'll be your shelter,
so just release.
Come to Me
and you'll find peace."

# DAY 16

## *Today's Verse*

"Let love be genuine. Abhor what is evil; hold fast
to what is good . . . Do not be overcome by evil,
but overcome evil with good." Romans 12:9, 21

## *Pause and Pray*

May we always love the way You've commanded us
to love, leaving all anger and wrath in Your hands so
that others only see Christ through us.

# The Great Exchange

To love is not a request—
it is given as a command.
We are to pray for all our persecutors.
We should always lend a helping hand.
Let's seek to always honor God
in all we say and do.
Having a servant's heart
is the call for me and you.
We should live in peace and harmony,
leaving wrath to God,
never trying to avenge ourselves
while walking on this sod.
Always do good to others
even when it doesn't make sense.
This is how they are called
to a place of repentance.
Never exchange evil for evil.
Always live like you should.
To overcome such evil
can only be done with good.

# DAY 17

## *Today's Verse*

"Blessed is the man who trusts in the LORD, whose trust is the LORD. He is like a tree planted by water, that sends out its roots by the stream, and does not fear when heat comes, for its leaves remain green, and is not anxious in the year of drought, for it does not cease to bear fruit." Jeremiah 17:7-8

## *Pause and Pray*

May our trust in You grow stronger, even in the pruning, and may we know that You are making us more fruitful.

# No Fear

All my hairs are numbered—
so are all my days—
by the One who knows me best
for He knows all my ways.
God knows every detail,
He has a perfect will.
He is magnificent and infinite
and He tells me to be still.
So I will lay my burdens down
at my Father's feet.
He will carry each one for me;
in Him I am complete.
His Providence has covered me
and every detail of my story,
so, whether things be good or bad
I give Him all the glory.

# DAY 18

## *Today's Verse*

"Because you have made the LORD your dwelling place—the Most High, who is my refuge—no evil shall be allowed to befall you, no plague come near your tent. For he will command his angels concerning you to guard you in all your ways. On their hands they will bear you up, lest you strike your foot against a stone. You will tread on the lion and the adder; The young lion and the serpent you will trample underfoot. 'Because he holds fast to me in love, I will deliver him; I will protect him, because he knows my name.'"

Psalm 91:9-14

## *Pause and Pray*

In these days where we are surrounded by darkness, we look to You for our protection. Thank you for the promise that you'll do just that.

# Everywhere I Go

God, I pray for Your protection
to guard me through all my days.
I pray for You to light my path
and keep me on the narrow way.
I pray You go each day before me,
stopping every evil foe.
Because You are my dwelling place,
I take You with me everywhere I go.
Command Your angels
where it concerns me
to guard me in all my ways.
May they hold me up before You
as I am calling on Your name.

# DAY 19

## *Today's Verse*

"If we confess our sins, he is faithful and just to forgive us our sins and to cleanse us from all unrighteousness."

1 John 1:9

## *Pause and Pray*

Thank you, Jesus, for dying on the cross to conquer sin once and for all. Thank you for filling us with Your Spirit to give us direction so that we always stay on the narrow path.

# Lights on the Dashboard

Our conscience is a warning system
pointing us to our sin,
like the lights on our dashboard
telling us something is wrong within.
There is a proper way to respond to this
if we will just hear it.
It is the one who beckons with our soul—
He is the Holy Spirit.
Our sins reflect so many things,
among them are guilt and shame,
but when we turn to Jesus Christ
He takes away our pain.
We can get to the root of this
and put our sins behind,
the perfect place to turn
is always 1 John 1:9.
Once we have repented
and fully agreed with the Lord,
He will restore our relationships,
far better than they were before.
Let us come with a humble heart
as we look upon His face,
for this is the only way
to receive His gift of grace.
Nothing is too big for Him
and nothing is too small.
Our sins are equal at the foot of the cross.
Jesus shed His blood for all.

---
# DAY 20
---

## Today's Verse

"Trust in the LORD with all your heart, and do not lean on your own understanding. In all your ways acknowledge him, and he will make straight your paths." Proverbs 3:5-6

## Pause and Pray

When answers to prayer do not look like we thought they would, help us to trust in Your plan and not in ourselves.

# He Speaks To Me

Others may find it quite odd
that my soul is hungry for God.
A still small voice is always heard
when I'm meditating on His Word.
It says, "be still and know you will be blessed,
for you are different from all the rest.
Do not seek them, looking for love.
What you need comes from above.
Trust in Me, be patient and find
perfect love of another kind.
Continue looking for Me—
when you look, you will find and you will see.
Always be loving and kind,
for vengeance has always been Mine.
Trust in Me with all your heart.
I have been with you right from the start.
I've never let go, so there's no reason to fear.
Through every trial I've always been near.
I am your Father and my Son is your friend;
We will be right with you until the very end."

---

# DAY 21

---

## Today's Verse

"For I delivered to you as of first importance what I also received: that Christ died for our sins in accordance with the Scriptures, that he was buried, that he was raised on the third day in accordance with the Scriptures." 1 Corinthians 15:3-4

## Pause and Pray

Hope begins at the foot of the cross. Joy begins at the empty tomb. We must always focus there.

# Looking Straight Ahead

The things in the rear-view mirror
cannot be undone,
they are merely a distraction
that takes our eyes off of the Son.
The devil sees what we have been through,
what is lingering in our past,
but let us look at the Man
with a love that always lasts.
We must let go of all the things
that are trying to keep us bound,
placing our faith in Jesus
where joy and peace are found.
Keeping our eyes on the road,
we must look straight ahead,
believing in the Man
that was raised up from the dead.
Behind us there is sorrow,
nothing but our sin.
So, we must choose to follow Jesus.
He is where eternal life begins.
He is the author and the finisher
of our growing faith.
So, we must turn our eyes to Jesus
who saved us by His grace.

---
# DAY 22
---

## *Today's Verse*

"For by grace you have been saved through faith.
And this is not your own doing; it is the gift of God,
not a result of works, so that no one may boast."

Ephesians 2:8-9

## *Pause and Pray*

The debt has been paid. There is nothing more to be
done. We don't have to earn it. Only believe!

# God's Grace

God's love goes much farther
then I could ever know.
For on the cross Jesus paid
for every debt I owed.
I'm not sure if you grasp
the words that I just said.
My sins have been forgiven
by the blood that Jesus bled.
The darkness from my past
has now been erased
by the Man who stands beside me
in every trial I face.
The love expressed by the Father,
who gave His only Son,
has made me now victorious
in the race that I must run.
So when you see the smile
and the expression on my face,
know that it is because of
my experience with God's grace
and the love of my Savior
who died at Calvary
and took on all my sins
so I could be set free.

# DAY 23

## *Today's Verse*

"I have blotted out your transgressions like a cloud
and your sins like mist; return to me, for I have
redeemed you." Isaiah 44:22

## *Pause and Pray*

There is nothing that can't be washed away by the
blood of Jesus Christ. Only He can make our way.
I praise Him for making the way for a sinner like me.

# When He Called My Name

It was loud and clear
when He called my name.
My eye was black,
my head hung in shame.
Surrounded by darkness,
I could see no way out.
I was battered and broken,
I only knew doubt.
I laid on my bed,
locked in my room.
Ashamed of my choices,
I felt nothing but doom.
I cried out to God—
it was late in the night—
demanding to be shown
to the Way, the Truth and the Life.
And the God full of mercy
and compassionate care
sent Jesus right in
to rescue me there.
It was not the same day
I called out His name—
but a thousand years or a day,
it's all one and the same.
He welcomed me in

with arms open wide.
When I ran to His Son
who suffered and died,
He declared my sins gone,
the slate was wiped clean.
He called out my name,
now He calls me redeemed.
I'll always remember
that night in my room,
surrounded by nothing
but sorrow and gloom,
when I called out for Jesus
and God made a plan
for me to make my way home
like only God can.

*"Now when I'm tossed
about to sea, I feel
His hand calm the
storm in me."*

- In the Stillness

# DAY 24

## *Today's Verse*

"Therefore, since we are surrounded by so great a cloud of witnesses, let us also lay aside every weight, and sin which clings so closely, and let us run with endurance the race that is set before us." Hebrews 12:1

## *Pause and Pray*

When we meet our Savior, we will stand among the great men of faith and in the presence of our Lord, the Man of greatest faith, hear the words, "well done." I look forward to that day. My prayer is you do too.

# Cheers from Heaven

Lord, my days keep getting harder here.
Oftentimes there's more bad than good.
I have to say in my finite mind
things aren't going like I thought they would.
But this doesn't mean Your plans have changed
or that You have forgotten me.
It only means that in this world
there are things far too big for me to see.
You are the Creator,
You made the heavens and the sea.
You named every single star,
You hold all eternity.
So, in my current circumstances,
I keep holding on to You.
You are the One with all the answers;
I can search Your Word for truth.
It tells me I must run a race
just like the heroes from before,
and if I do it with endurance
there will be heavenly rewards.
I can't say that this is easy,
I must admit that I am weak,
but I'm holding on to Jesus.
He is the Truth that I seek.
He tells me I can do this,
that I'll never walk alone,
for I am being cheered for
until the day I reach His throne.

# DAY 25

*Today's Verse*

"And he awoke and rebuked the wind and said to the sea, 'Peace! Be still!' And the wind ceased, and there was a great calm." Mark 4:39

*Pause and Pray*

There is one thing that is certain in the Christian life—we will have tribulations. When we least expect it, our seas will begin to rage and waves will seem to be taking us under. But when we put our faith in the Man who commands even the raging seas, He will keep us in His perfect peace.

# Call on the Name of Jesus

In the middle of our storm
Jesus is our source of peace.
He spoke the words, "be still,"
and calmed the raging seas.
Nothing can compare to Him,
even the winds respond to His commands,
and He is our protection.
He holds on to us with loving hands.
His love for us He did display
upon the cross at Calvary,
and for all who call out His name
He gives the promise of eternity.
We know the man that spoke the words
that calmed the raging sea.
Remember that His plans are good
and that He will do the same for you and me.
So, no matter what our struggles are
or what we are going through,
we can call on the name of Jesus
and He'll do the same for me and you.

---

# DAY 26

---

## *Today's Verse*

"Keep your life free from love of money, and be
content with what you have, for he has said,
'I will never leave you nor forsake you.' So we can
confidently say, 'The Lord is my helper; I will
not fear; What can man do to me?'" Hebrews 13:5-6

## *Pause and Pray*

God's Word gives us everything we need for anything
that we face. When facing any adversity, we must pick
up our sword. The battle is hard, but the battle is good
when we are well-equipped.

# Faith

We trust Him with the little things—
that is the easy part.
But do we truly trust Him
when our lives are falling apart?
God is always faithful—
we all know that this is true.
Peeking into our past
shows just what He can do.
He's carried us in His hand
through every trial we have faced,
but because we are human,
fear is not erased.
We must remember when we're tested
like we were before
that fear is from the enemy,
it does not come from the Lord.
So, when we are carrying
more than we think we can bare,
we must search through the Scriptures.
We will find our comfort there.

---

# DAY 27

---

## *Today's Verse*

"And we know that for those who love God all things work together for good, for those who are called according to his purpose." Romans 8:28

## *Pause and Pray*

It doesn't matter how ugly or how painful things look on the outside. We must trust in the One who turns ashes to beauty and pain into hope and healing. Even in the hard times, He always knows what's best.

# Made Completely Whole

Sometimes there are many things
I cannot understand,
sometimes I fail to remember
who has the master plan.
I get caught up in worry
for things I can't control,
failing to remember
it's you, Lord,
who makes me whole.
I'm so thankful for your Word
and the promises held within,
knowing that You love me
and You always call me friend.
Your plans are always good
and there will never be defeat.
You are the author of my story,
in you I am complete.
Jesus died for my sins,
now I have been sealed.
Your Word says it's by His stripes
that I am completely healed.
Until the day Your plan is manifested
and You have come to reveal it,
I will walk in victory
through Your Holy Spirit.

---

# DAY 28

---

## *Today's Verse*

"But he said to me, 'My grace is sufficient for you,
for my power is made perfect in weakness.' Therefore
I will boast all the more gladly of my weaknesses, so
that the power of Christ may rest upon me."

2 Corinthians 12:9

## *Pause and Pray*

Oftentimes, weakness is frowned upon by the world.
But as believers, we know that in our weakness God
shows His strength. What an awesome God we serve!
He puts His power on display when we no longer have
the strength within ourselves to keep going. He is
glorified through our weaknesses!

# A Diamond in The Rough

I used to think it was punishment
when sifted by the enemy,
unable to always recognize
It was part of His purpose for me.
Every single battle
and every single foe
had a special purpose
that I didn't know.
All of the pressures
that I was going through
were not only for my good
but for His glory too.
He's been making me and shaping me
to look more like His Son,
and I'm sure to face more trials
until my race down here is run.
Because just like the diamond
that shines so brilliantly,
I must endure more pressure
for Jesus's light to shine through me.
What a new perspective
that clears up my uncertainty
that through every single trial
His light shines brighter through me!
Now when I have a thorn
ripping in my flesh,
I can trust my Father.
His way is always best.

---

# DAY 29

---

## *Today's Verse*

"Blessed be the God and Father of our Lord Jesus
Christ, the Father of mercies and God of all comfort,
who comforts us in all our affliction, so that we may
be able to comfort those who are in any affliction, with
the comfort with which we ourselves are comforted
by God. For as we share abundantly in Christ's
sufferings, so through Christ we share abundantly in
comfort too. If we are afflicted, it is for your comfort
and salvation; and if we are comforted, it is for your
comfort, which you experience when you patiently
endure the same sufferings that we suffer. Our hope
for you is unshaken, for we know that as you share in
our sufferings, you will also share in our comfort."

2 Corinthians 1:3-7

## *Pause and Pray*

No one wants to suffer. Suffering is unpleasant.
Look what happened to our Savior. If suffering
makes us look more like Him, then it is an honor to
suffer for Him. No one understands our pain more
than, the Lamb of God!

# Suffering like Our Savior

We have all experienced
in many kinds of sufferings,
and although they were uncomfortable
they changed so many things.
We grew in our sanctification,
making us more holy,
and as we came to the throne of grace
we learned to do it boldly.
No one has ever suffered more
than the Man upon the cross,
the One who made the way
for everyone who is lost.
So, remember in all the battles
we are sure to have to go through
suffering like our Savior
is an honor for me and you.
For in every single trial
we are called to face,
we look more like our Savior
and His amazing grace.

---
# DAY 30
---

## *Today's Verse*

"My mouth is filled with your praise, and with your glory all the day." Psalm 71:8

## *Pause and Pray*

There is no other name in heaven or on earth above the name of Jesus. I will praise Him in my failures and in my darkest valleys solely because He is worthy! My circumstances will change, but my God never will.

# Jesus Magnified

Lord, I surrender to You my thoughts
because of the damage they can do.
I surrender to You my tongue
when my words are not pleasing to You.
I surrender to You my heart
for it is wicked and misunderstood,
and I ask for You to restore me
to what is pure and lovely and good.
I asked that You completely change me
into the image of Your Son
until my race on Earth is through,
always being faithful to the run.
When others look my way
may I reflect my Savior's light.
May I become invisible
so that Jesus will be in full sight.
May everything that I say,
may everything that I do,
always remain in focus
as I choose to glorify You.

---

# DAY 31

---

*Today's Verse*

> "For he will command his angels concerning you, to guard you in all your ways." Psalm 91:11

*Pause and Pray*

> How comforting to know that the Lord commands His angels to guard us! Notice that He doesn't suggest that they stand by and watch. I always feel safer knowing that His angels are guarding me. Throughout my life my angels have had an endless job. I'm so thankful that they were faithful to their calling.

# Angels Everywhere

Sitting here,
I appear alone.
But there is a presence
that is unknown.
The comfort in
this room today
must be angels
guiding my way.
They've been sent
from God above
to remind me of
his unfailing love.
And in the midst
of uncertainty,
they stand wing tip to wing tip
guarding me.
They go before me
to keep me safe
until I reach
the Pearly Gates.
They give me comfort.
They cast out fear.
When I need them,
they're always near.
They're sent from heaven
to show He cares.
My angels are with me
everywhere.

# DAY 32

## *Today's Verse*

"Fear not, for I am with you; be not dismayed,
for I am your God; I will strengthen you,
I will help you, I will uphold you with my
righteous right hand." Isaiah 41:10

## *Pause and Pray*

Our confidence in the Lord should grow, since
we know that He is always holding us up in His
righteous right hand. He alone is our source of
strength and comfort.

# In His Hands

Just how big are His arms
when they are open wide?
Just how big is His palm
that He holds all of us inside?
Do His arms outreach the heavens?
Will His hand also hold the sea?
Can the One who named the stars
care that much for me?
He says He is my Shepherd,
full of tender loving care,
and in my darkest moments
He assures me that He is there.
Every single battle
has never been fought alone.
The victory has been won
by the One who sits upon the throne.
The God of wrath and judgement
is the God of mercy and grace.
The proof is more than evident
because His Son died in my place.
He was nailed to a cross,
his blood dripping from a tree,
covering all my sins,
proving His love for me.
His Word is full of promises
and every one is true.
He's not only holding me;
His hands are also holding you.

# DAY 33

## *Today's Verse*

"Abide in me, and I in you. As the branch cannot bear fruit by itself, unless it abides in the vine, neither can you, unless you abide in me. I am the vine; you are the branches. Whoever abides in me and I in him, he it is that bears much fruit, for apart from me you can do nothing." John 15:4-5

## *Pause and Pray*

I have tried more times than I can count to do life on my own. It was disastrous every single time. But when I abide in Jesus, He makes things happen that I could have never imagined. The best example that I can give you is this devotional you are currently reading. From start to finish, it has come from abiding in Jesus.

# Abiding in You

I can't do anything without You
except fall completely apart.
I want to bring You glory
and to never break Your heart.
But when I woke this morning
with tears streaming down my face,
I could not help but question
why You brought me to this place.
My circumstances are harder
than I thought they would ever be.
I am completely defeated.
Are these the words of the enemy?
I know that You abide in me
because I abide in You,
and today I'm calling on Your name
for all I am going through.
Help me hold my head up.
Please don't let me fall.
In the midst of this uncertainty,
it's on Your name I call.
Jesus is my strength,
so there's nothing I can't do.
This might be too hard for me,
but it is not too hard for You.
Strengthen me from within,
bring me back to peace.
These things that I cannot carry
I must now release.
God is the Almighty,
His Son is always by my side.
Jesus is the strong vine
in which I must abide.

# DAY 34

## *Today's Verse*

"Finally, be strong in the Lord and in the strength of his might." Ephesians 6:10

## *Pause and Pray*

When we find ourselves faced with circumstances out of our control, we put our trust in the One who controls our circumstances. He alone is our strength in every uncertainty.

# To the Lover of My Soul

I've been sitting at Your feet now
for going on a couple of years,
and in that time, You've had to catch
so many of my tears.
You've been faithful to bring me through
every trial that I've faced,
but this one feels much different
like it cannot be erased.
Sin certainly has its consequences—
that's been plain to see—
and I thank You that my chains are gone
and that You set me free.
I open up my heart to You.
I've heard it's getting weak.
For a moment I let that bring me down,
life started to look bleak.
But I remember the word You gave me
to focus on this year,
so I draw my strength from You.
Please cast out all my fear.
Put your glory on display,
show Your power and Your might,
and as I face this trial
I will hold on to You tight.
You're more than just my friend,
You're the lover of my soul.
And even if my heart is weak,
You've still made it completely whole.
My heart belongs to You now,
do with it as You please.
No matter what the outcome is,
with You I can face life's raging seas.

---

# DAY 35

---

## Today's Verse

"But Moses said to the LORD, "Oh, my Lord,
I am not eloquent, either in the past or since you
have spoken to your servant, but I am slow of
speech and of tongue." Then the LORD said to him,
'Who has made man's mouth? Who makes him mute,
or deaf, or seeing, or blind? Is it not I, the LORD?
Now therefore go, and I will be with your mouth and
teach you what you shall speak.'" Exodus 4:10-12

## Pause and Pray

Every believer is useful to God. He has equipped us
all with unique gifts and abilities. We must always use
whatever those talents are to glorify God. It matters!
Eternity is at stake! Listen to Him.

# He Never Gives Up

Where would I be
if He hadn't moved first?
I'd be without hunger.
I'd be without thirst.
I was missing the mark,
blowing it each day.
Where would I be
if He hadn't come my way?
The God of second chances
who knew all my sins,
the One I betrayed
changed me from within.
He says I am useful,
I just can't understand
how I could ever be part
of His glorified plan.
On any old day
His voice can be heard.
His ways can be common
or completely absurd.
Only God can erase
such a horrid past.
His power is limitless,
He gives freedom that lasts.
It doesn't even matter
what other folks see—
being pleasing to God
is all that matters to me!
God doesn't give up
I hope you can see;
He can certainly use you
if He can use me.

# DAY 36

## *Today's Verse*

"But they who wait for the LORD shall renew their strength; they shall mount up with wings like eagles; they shall run and not be weary; they shall walk and not faint." Isaiah 40:31

## *Pause and Pray*

As we walk through each day, Lord, hold on to us tightly, renewing our strength so that we never grow weary. Whether we walk, run, or soar like the eagle, we draw our strength from You, learning more about who you are and portraying Your character to others. When we begin to soar like the majestic eagle, may we always remember that You gave us our wings.

# Know You More

I know You sent Your Son
to take on all my sins
and that at the foot of the Cross
is where eternal life begins.
I know that You give me grace
when I fail along the way.
I know You give me new mercies
to make it through each day.
I feel Your steadfast love
surround me more and more
and when my faith grows dim
I look back at all the things you've done before.
You are the Almighty
and Your Son calls me His Friend.
You are the Alpha and the Omega,
You are the beginning and the end.
You are all my comfort.
With You it's on eagle's wings I soar.
I love You with all my heart;
My only desire is to know You more.
Please go with me each day
guiding my steps across this land.
I always want You with me
walking hand in hand.

---

# DAY 37

---

## *Today's Verse*

"So if there is any encouragement in Christ, any comfort from love, any participation in the Spirit, any affection and sympathy, complete my joy by being of the same mind, having the same love, being in full accord and of one mind." Philippians 2:1-2

## *Pause and Pray*

Fill us each day with Your Spirit, putting to death our flesh. Help us walk in a manner that is pleasing to you. Control our thoughts and emotions. Put a guard on our tongues. Fill us full of joy that only comes from You.

# I Want To Look Like You

On the days I hurt
and I'm filled with pain,
on the days I wonder
if you still know my name,
help me to be content
in everything I do,
knowing that all Your promises
never lose their truth.
Fill me with Your Spirit,
encourage me with Your love,
restore me back to joy
that only comes from above.
Always protect my thoughts.
It's You I long to find,
hoping to be of one accord,
my thoughts looking like Your mind.
When I search Your Word
may I see Your heart.
I long to be more holy
from You I never want to part.
In everything I say,
in everything I do,
may I always look
more and more like You.

---

# DAY 38

---

## *Today's Verse*

"You shall have no other gods before me." Exodus 20:3

## *Pause and Pray*

Your Word speaks of idolatry more than any other sin. Keep a guard on our hearts by helping us to put You first in everything we do—keeping our motives pure. May we look to Your Word each day to guide our path and light our way.

# First of All

Your Word does so many things
I wish I could express.
It gives me hope and restores my soul;
through it I'm truly blessed.
Whenever I am persecuted
and begin to feel down,
it reminds me if I stay the course
one day I'll have a crown.
It teaches me biblical standards
on how to live my life.
It brings me into perfect peace
in a world that is full of strife.
If I ever feel alone,
 or like I am unheard,
I find encouragement for my soul
when I open up Your Word.
It keeps me on the narrow path
so that I may not fall.
 It teaches me each day in life
that You come first of all.

---
# DAY 39
---

*Today's Verse*

"Behold, I am with you always, to the end of the age."

Matthew 28:20

*Pause and Pray*

We are never alone. May we always feel Your presence because You are always there in everything we face.

# Always

We all know His plans are good
and that His Word is true.
We've all read about His miracles
so we know there's nothing He can't do.
We've been told so many times to trust
and not to be afraid;
He will use all of our circumstances
for His glory to be displayed.
So we put our faith in Jesus Christ,
then choose to follow Him
and hold on to Him tightly
when life's road gets very dim.
Sometimes promises don't come quickly,
oftentimes we have to wait,
but we must not grow weary in doing good
because our Savior is never late.
When He spoke His words
He made it very clear
that we would never be alone.
That's why we should not fear!
So even in the valley
on our darkest days
He said He would be with us.
And when He said it, He said, "Always."
We must thank Him for our trials
knowing He is right there,
making us to look like Himself—
that's how much He cares!

---

# DAY 40

---

## *Today's Verse*

"And whatever you do, in word or deed, do
everything in the name of the Lord Jesus, giving
thanks to God the Father through Him."

Colossians 3:17

## *Pause and Pray*

Lord, I pray for the reader. For fellow believers,
I pray for encouragement where it's needed and
comfort for broken hearts. But Lord, more than
anything I pray that, no matter the circumstance,
You are glorified in it and through it always.

And, Lord, if anyone who has read this book does
not have a relationship with you, please show them
Your mercy and give them the grace to ask You to
save them. Pour out Your love, and teach them
to walk in Your ways.

# I Prayed for You

I said a prayer for you today
and I know God surely heard,
for everything I asked for you
came straight from His Word.
I prayed for your protection,
that He'd cast out all your fear.
I prayed that He would hold you close
because you are so dear.
I prayed that He would lift you up
and never let you fall.
I prayed that He would give you peace
and answer you each time you call.
I prayed you'd always feel His love
and that you never feel that down
and when this life is over
I prayed that you would have a crown.
I prayed He'd give you patience
with all you're going through
and I prayed you'd always honor Him
In everything you do.

# Acknowledgments

All praise, honor, and glory to our Father and His Son, Jesus Christ, who changed me from the inside out and gave me every gift that I have. Without them I would be nothing.

Also, I thank my parents, biblical counselors, and friends who never gave up on me and believed in me when I didn't believe in myself. You all know who you are.

Special thanks to the late "Papa," Daryle Hembree, the first person to show me the love of Christ and his family who were instrumental in my rescue.

Also, to my children, my brothers and their families who were hurt along the way. Sometimes forgiving is the hardest thing we do. I love you all.

# About the Author

Stacy Brantner was born in Toccoa, Georgia, in 1974, and spent her early years in the loving care of her grandparents, surrounded by cherished memories with aunts, uncles, and cousins. At the age of ten, she moved to Travelers Rest, South Carolina, where she would grow up and spend most of her life.

Her love for poetry began in her youth, sparked by the emotions of her first broken heart. Though she wrote often, her poems remained hidden—and were eventually lost as life took her down difficult roads. Everything changed on July 7, 2010, when she was hit by a drunk driver. The injuries required neck fusion surgery and long-term pain management, which led to an overprescription of oxycodone. This began a decade-long battle with addiction and the many sins that held her captive.

On September 12, 2023, Stacy entered The Summit of Fort Payne (Alabama), an intensive discipleship program that would transform her life. On her second day in the program, she placed all her hope and trust in Jesus Christ and committed to following Him. God broke her chains of addiction, set her free from the strongholds in her life, and soon renewed her passion for poetry—this time to glorify Him.

Today, Stacy draws inspiration from the truth and promises of God's Word, finding it sufficient for every circumstance. Without Christ as Lord of her life, this book would not exist. She has prayed over every reader of *In the Stillness*, and it is her deepest desire that these Scripture-inspired poems bring you the same hope and comfort she has found in Him.

www.ingramcontent.com/pod-product-compliance
Lightning Source LLC
Chambersburg PA
CBHW051325120626
46547CB00015B/2403